SUPPORTING THOSE WHO SERVE OUR NATION

jctm.us/a2c2

Advanced AI Command Course

Prompt Engineering

By ML Brei

www.jctm.us/a2c2

Published by Meripoint Books LLC; P.O. Box 1512; Williamsburg, Virginia 23185

Joint Computer Technologies & Training Management (JCTM) is an 8(a) certified, Service Disabled Veteran Owned Small Business (SDVOSB) with VA certification, focused on bringing repair and healing to ordinary people as we continue to serve our great nation, its service members, and fellow veterans by supporting specialized programs across the Department of Defense (DoD) and National Intelligence Agencies. JCTM specializes in Command, Control, Communications, Computers, Cyber, Intelligence, Surveillance, & Reconnaissance (C5ISR) technology integration and support services, in addition to software development.

For permissions or inquiries, contact JCTM, LLC. 16710 Tulloch Road; Charlotte, NC 28278

This guidebook was developed with the assistance of AI tools, including ChatGPT (Feb 2024 version, OpenAI), for brainstorming ideas, answering technical questions, and formatting tables. All AI-generated content was carefully reviewed, edited, and verified to ensure accuracy and maintain human oversight. The final content reflects the author's expertise and judgment, with AI serving as a supportive tool rather than an autonomous creator.

Cover design by ML Brei assisted by DALLE-3

Paperback ISBN 978-1960808097
Printed in the United States of America.

Contents

Agenda

Welcome and Systems Orientation

Task List Demo, Intro to AI, Prompt Engineering, Design Process

Principles of Prompt Design

Augmented Prompting, Practice, Retrieval Augmented Generation

Prompt Hierarchy & Direct Instruction Example

Zero-shot Prompting, Brainstorming, Practice

One-shot, N-shot Prompting, & Practice

   5-min. Break

Conceptual Overview

Prompt Chaining

Persona Pattern, Audience Pattern, Practice

Template Pattern Practice

   30-min. Lunch

Flipped Interaction Pattern, Practice

Game Play Pattern, Practice

Semantic Filter

   5-min. Break

Reflection

The Right Use of AI (Limitations, Framework for Ethical Use)

Hands-On Practice

Conclusion

Additional Demos & Questions

Introduction

Artificial Intelligence (AI) is a broad field that spans multiple disciplines, all aimed at developing tools that simulate human intelligence by learning, reasoning, and self-correcting. The ultimate goal is to perform tasks traditionally requiring human cognition.

A key subfield of AI is Natural Language Processing (NLP), which includes natural language understanding (NLU) and natural language generation (NLG). This workshop focuses on working with state-of-the-art NLG systems, also known as Generative AI (GenAI).

The overarching goal of GenAI is to generate human-like language or enable machines to engage in natural conversation. Technological breakthroughs such as the transformer model (introduced in 2017) and OpenAI's ChatGPT (released in 2022) marked pivotal moments—ushering in the first publicly-known instance of a machine capable of responding fluently in human language.

At the heart of these advancements is **machine learning**, the driving force behind modern artificial intelligence. Machine learning refers to algorithms that enable computers to "learn" from data and make predictions based on patterns within that data. In this context, learning is narrowly defined—it means recognizing patterns in data in relation to a specific goal and improving this recognition through repeated exposure.

But LLMs go beyond simple pattern recognition. As they scale, they exhibit emergent capabilities—unexpected behaviors that arise once the model surpasses a certain threshold of complexity.

For example, larger LLMs have demonstrated the ability to:

- Translate between languages without being explicitly trained on bilingual datasets.

- Follow complex instructions and reason through problems, even solving riddles and logic puzzles.

- Write functional programming code, even in languages they were never fine-tuned on.

- Engage in few-shot learning, meaning they can generalize from just a few examples rather than requiring extensive retraining.

These capabilities make LLMs not just advanced, but transformative. However, because emergent behaviors arise from the sheer scale and depth of training, their exact mechanisms remain an active area of research.

In this workshop, you'll learn how to design prompts that **elicit these emergent capabilities**, allowing you to leverage LLMs effectively for your own needs. The process of designing prompts to achieve specific outcomes is known as **Prompt Engineering**, and mastering this discipline will enable you to unlock the full potential of GenAI.

The Prompt Engineering Design Process

Prompt Engineering transcends the mere construction of prompts; it requires a blend of domain knowledge, understanding the AI model, and a methodical approach to tailor prompts for different contexts.

Xavier Amatriain, VP of AI/ML at Google

Prompt engineering is distinct from *prompt crafting*.

Prompt crafting is the spontaneous creation of a direct instruction or query to an LLM for immediate results. For example: *"Please provide an executive summary of the following text."* This prompt would likely generate a usable summary of variable length, potentially with bullet points. While prompt crafting can yield useful results, they may not always be reliable, repeatable, or precisely what you intended.

Prompt engineering, on the other hand, is a process that effectively "programs" LLMs to produce content that aims to be both repeatable and reliable while fulfilling a specific function. As a process, it is both iterative and results-focused. Let's look closer at what this process entails.

An Iterative Process

Prompt engineering is not a linear process with a defined start and finish, but rather a continuous cycle of improvement. The goal is to refine the instructions given to an LLM to achieve a desired outcome. This requires continuous adjustments based on the LLM's output, feedback from experts, and analysis of performance metrics.

We can identify six main steps in the process:

1. **Problem Definition:** The first step is to clearly define the goals you want to achieve with the LLM and the specific tasks it should perform. This also involves identifying potential challenges related to the tasks or domain.

2. **Domain Understanding and Data Analysis:** After defining the problem, we combine input from domain experts and gather relevant data to inform prompt design. This step involves analyzing existing documentation, project specifications, and research papers to identify patterns, keywords, and other relevant information.

3. **Prompt Design and Technique Selection:** At this point, we draft the initial prompt based on the defined objectives, domain knowledge, and data analysis. The prompt should be clear, specific,

contextually relevant, and targeted to address the identified challenges. The choice of prompting techniques and/or patterns employed will depend on the complexity of the task.

4. **Evaluation and Refinement:** Once the initial prompt is designed, we test it with the LLM, and evaluate the output. This includes checking for accuracy, relevance, conciseness, potential biases, and alignment with the defined goals. Based on this evaluation, we refine the prompt and improve it iteratively. This might involve adjusting the wording, adding more context, or switching to a different prompting technique.

5. **Expert Feedback and Collaboration:** Throughout the process, we seek feedback from subject matter experts and collaborate with them to improve the prompt and ensure the LLM's output meets the desired standards.

6. **Documentation:** As we refine the prompt and see improvements in the LLM output, we document what we have learned, what succeeded, what didn't. This documentation serves as a valuable resource for future prompt engineering endeavors and helps in sharing knowledge within the field.

The Process

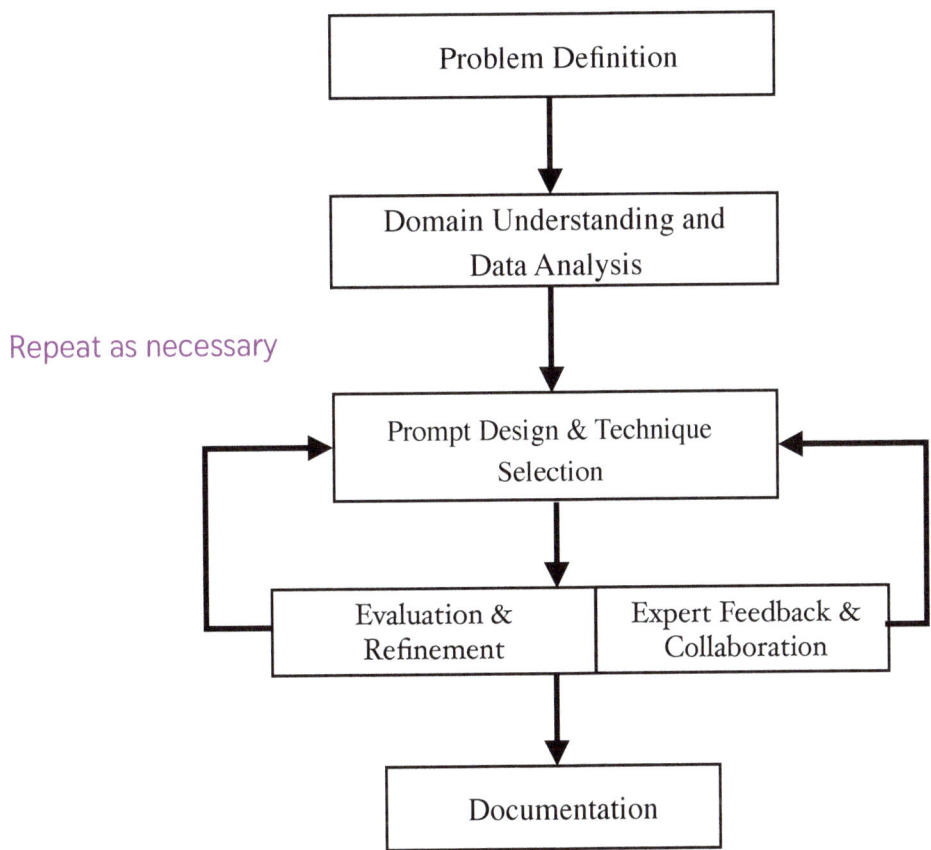

This diagram is a simplified representation as the process typically involves a dynamic interplay between different stages. For instance, evaluating the LLM output might highlight the need to revisit the problem definition or the data analysis stage. Similarly, expert feedback could prompt changes in both prompt design and technique selection. This continuous feedback loop and the iterative nature of refinement are crucial aspects of prompt engineering, enabling the development of increasingly effective prompts that harness the full potential of LLMs.

Key Takeaways:

- **Prompt crafting** is quick and effective for ad hoc tasks but lacks repeatability.

- **Prompt engineering** is a structured, iterative process focused on **reliable, optimized performance**.

- Effective prompt engineering requires problem definition, data gathering, testing, refinement, expert feedback, and documentation.

- Using Prompt Patterns helps structure prompts for optimized and reliable results.

- Techniques such as augmented prompting, few-shot learning, prompt chaining, contextual prompting, and reflective analysis help improve outcomes over time.

By treating prompt engineering as a **methodical discipline**, rather than a trial-and-error exercise, we can harness the full potential of LLMs while ensuring **consistency, precision, and alignment with intended goals**.

Prompting Principles

What you write and how you write it directly impacts the quality of the output.

Jules White, Vanderbilt University

All prompts should follow three principles:

1. **Clarity**: A clear statement expresses intent and is unambiguous. This gives the model a clear focal point. To test for clarity, answer these questions:

   1. Is the intent or direction of the prompt obvious?

   2. Is it unambiguous?

   3. Does the model know what aspect of the prompt to focus on?

2. **Specificity**: All prompts should include specific details—context, boundaries, scope, etc. Even if the prompt has an intent (clarity), if it doesn't include specifics, then the prompt is too broad. The response will be equally broad. A good rule of thumb is "make your prompt as specific as you want the response to be."

   A second aspect of specificity is **relevancy**. Refrain from adding irrelevant details to the prompt. Research shows that irrelevant data causes the LLM to randomly prioritize the sections of the prompt they will respond to. The response may be less accurate or off-target.

3. **Output Format**: We want to tell the LLM both the specific details to include in the response and how to structure the response. If we don't tell it exactly the information we want, the response may not include the details we need. Likewise, without specifying the format, the model will use a default format for the output, typically a paragraph or bulleted list. There is no reason to limit yourself to the default formats. Depending on the model that you are using, the range of outputs it knows how to create is impressive.

The table on the next page, **Capabilities and Output of Frontier Models**, gives you an idea of the range of outputs you might request from advanced models.

6

Capabilities and Outputs
of Frontier Large Language Models (LLMs)

The skill of the user in writing the prompts and knowing what can be done with this tool is incredibly important.

Jules White, Vanderbilt University

Category	Capabilities/Output Format
Textual	Generating summaries, essays, stories, poems, jokes, explanations, paraphrasing, question-answering, translations (over 100 languages including Spanish, French, German, Chinese, Japanese, Russian, Arabic, Hindi, and Swahili), creative writing, and brainstorming ideas.
Document	Drafting formal reports, legal documents, business plans, curriculum outlines, research proposals, lesson plans, meeting agendas, memos, and resumes.
Code Output	Producing scripts, algorithms, and software snippets in languages including Python, C++, JavaScript, HTML, SQL, Java, R, MATLAB, Bash, C, C#, Ruby, PHP, Perl, Swift, Kotlin, Scala, Go, TypeScript, Fortran, COBOL, Shell scripting.
Visualizations	Generating bar charts, line graphs, scatter plots, pie charts, histograms, and diagrams (via tools). Crafting flowcharts, system architecture diagrams, entity-relationship diagrams, timelines, Gantt charts, and organizational charts (text or tool-aided).
Interactive	Designing interactive quizzes and games, conversational simulations, branching stories, and educational scenarios.
Data Output & File Export	Generating structured data, tables, statistical summaries, data transformations, and descriptive analysis. Producing content for export to formats including PDF, CSV, JSON, XML, HTML, markdown, and Word-compatible formats. Supporting tools and applications include Visual Studio, Obsidian, Jupyter Notebook, and others for enhanced productivity.
Multimedia	Creating video scripts, audio scripts, storyboards, and textual inputs for animations or multimedia projects.
Specializations	Creating domain-specific outputs like medical analyses, legal explanations, business strategies, scientific research, and engineering plans.

ASCII	Generating ASCII art, tables, diagrams, banners, or symbolic representations.
Productivity	Drafting to-do lists, project timelines, task prioritization, goal tracking, and productivity techniques.
Creative Design	Generating ideas for fashion, interior design, branding concepts, UX designs, and artistic projects.
Mathematical	Solving equations, generating formulas, creating proofs, simplifying expressions, and producing LaTeX code for mathematical documentation.
Language Tools & Editing	Grammar correction, style analysis, tone adjustment, readability scoring, and linguistic comparisons.
Food/ Entertainment	Creating trivia, jokes, riddles, horoscopes, games, menus, recipes, and travel itineraries.
Presentation	Generating slides (textual outlines), presentation scripts, pitch decks, structured speech formats, and PowerPoint-compatible content.
Research	Providing literature reviews, bibliographies, reference generation (in formats such as MLA, APA, Chicago, Harvard, IEEE, and AMA), and research summaries.
Educational Tools	Generating lesson plans, teaching aids, activities, assessments, and visual aids tailored to various age groups or expertise levels. Explaining concepts, providing examples, offering definitions, creating study guides, generating quizzes, and recommending resources for self-learning.
Personalization	Drafting personalized emails, letters, invitations, and customized content for specific audiences or individuals.
Application Integration	Supporting productivity and creativity with tools like Excel (data processing), Google Docs (collaboration), CMS tools like WordPress, and integration with APIs for automation. Creating interactive and embedded visualizations compatible with Tableau, Power BI, and other dashboard tools.
AI Tools	Aiding AI workflows by designing prompts for APIs, generating datasets for fine-tuning, and providing insights for using AI effectively.
Accessibility	Producing text-to-speech outputs, screen-reader-friendly content, captions/subtitles, and adapting outputs for improved accessibility.
Content Adaptation	Customizing content to suit specific audiences, adjusting for literacy levels, age groups, or professional expertise.
Simulation Tools	Developing scenarios for decision-making, training, role-playing, and interactive learning environments.

Large Language Model Fundamentals

Before introducing specific prompting techniques and patterns, we begin with a conceptual overview of how large language models (LLM) function.

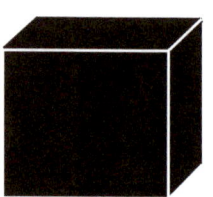 This is an LLM: a black box.

The purpose of this box is to predict the next word.

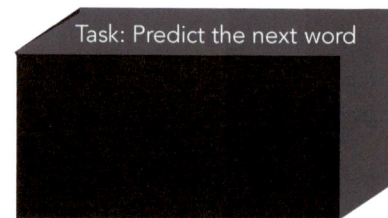

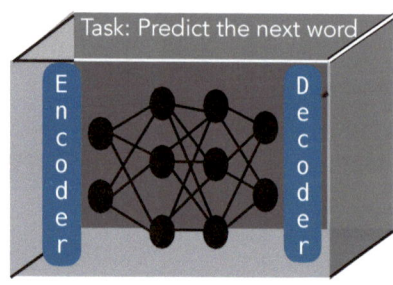 Inside the box, there is an "engine" composed of many units. The most important is the neural network (model) that has a transformer architecture. Other components include an encoder and decoder.

The box isn't ready for humans yet. First, the neural network has to be trained. All information on the internet has been scraped and used to train the model. This essentially feeds the model a vast amount of text data, allowing it to recognize patterns, relationships between words, and even the underlying meaning of sentences.

The model does not memorize the text—it learns statistical probabilities: it predicts the most likely next word based on context rather than recalling exact phrases from its training data.

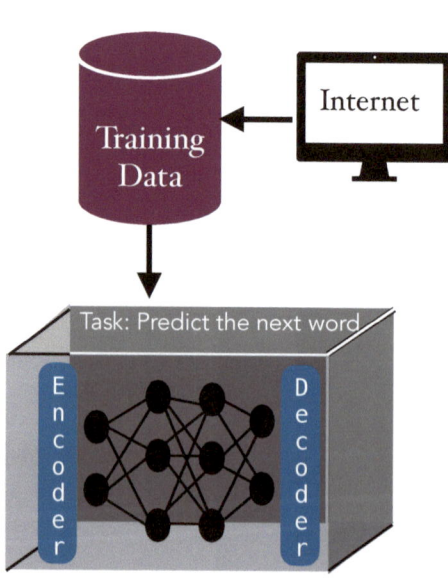

Once the neural network has been trained, the black box is still not quite ready. It must go through a process called fine-tuning, where it is adjusted with additional curated data using human annotators to refine its responses for specific tasks, such as answering questions, summarizing text, or even generating creative stories.

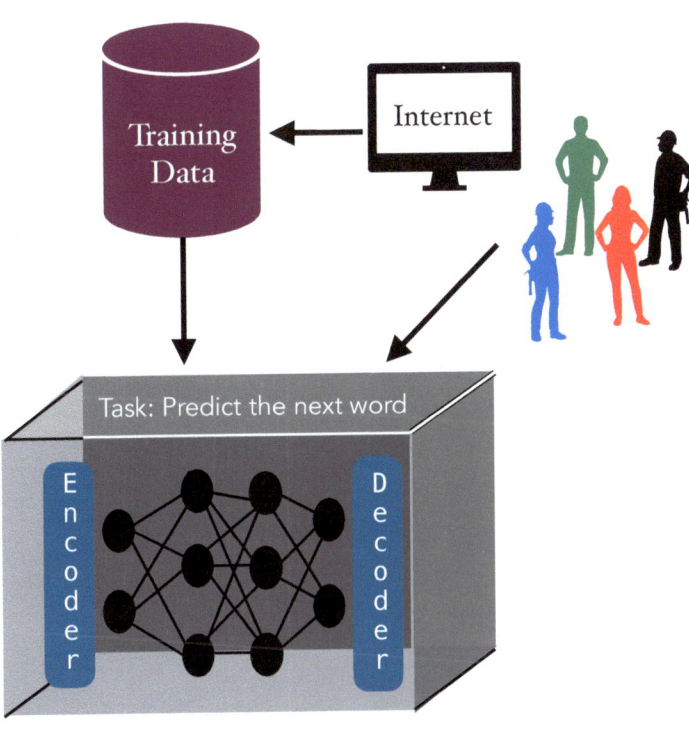

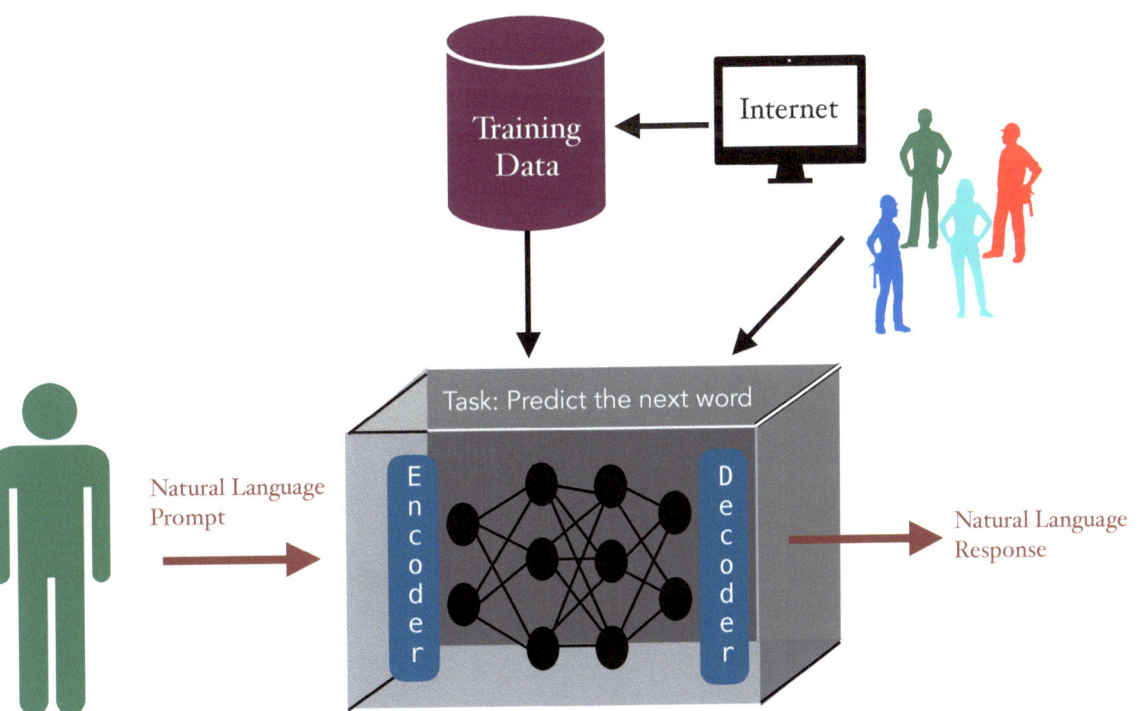

Now the box is ready for humans. A human types a natural language statement, a prompt, into the black box.

The words of the prompt are broken in tokens. The tokens are encoded (by the encoder) into numeric values and passed through the neural network. This network processes the input by analyzing the relationships between tokens and predicting the most probable next token based on its training data.

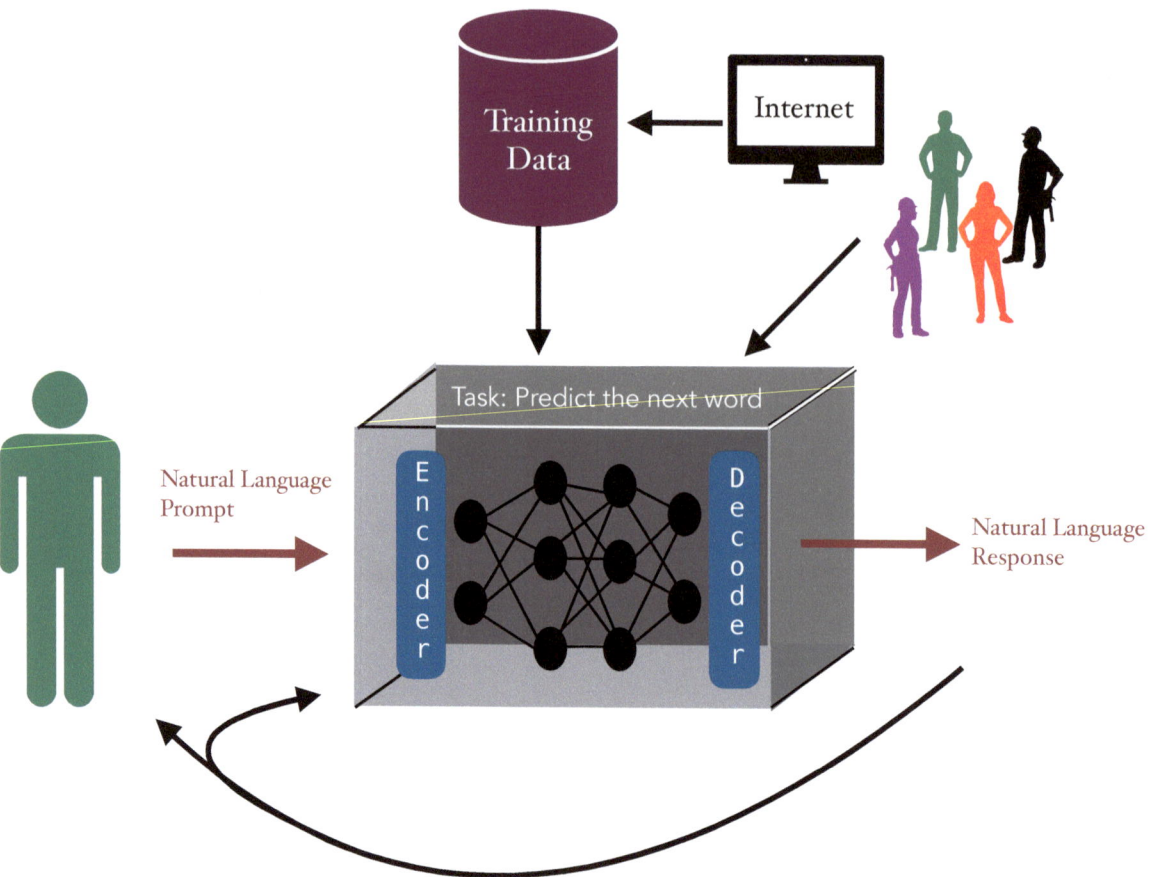

Inside the black box, the encoded tokens travel through multiple **layers** of the transformer model. Each layer refines the model's understanding of context using **self-attention**, a mechanism that determines which parts of the input are most relevant to predicting the next token. This allows the model to capture complex dependencies in language, even across long sentences or paragraphs.

Once the processing is complete, the model produces a ranked list of possible next tokens, selecting the most likely one based on probabilities. These tokens are then **decoded back into human-readable words**, forming a response that is displayed to the user.

When the user submits a second prompt, the original prompt and its response are appended to the new prompt. This entire sequence is fed back into the model, allowing it to generate a response based on the full conversation history within its **context window.**

Each time the user prompts the model, the prior exchanges (prompts and responses) are included in the input, enabling the model to maintain conversational continuity. However, this process continues **only until the context window is full**. Once the context window limit is reached, older parts of the conversation are typically **discarded from the beginning** to make space for new input. The model will no longer have access to the earliest exchanges.

Important takeaway:

From the outside, the black box seems almost magical—it takes in a human question or statement and generates a fluent response. But inside, it's all about numbers, probabilities, and patterns, turning raw input into meaningful language through sheer computational power.

Remember: Your prompt is the beginning of the response.

The Prompt Hierarchy

Generative AI was taught to respond to patterns in human language.

Jules White, Vanderbilt University

User prompts for large language models (LLMs) can be categorized into two broad types: Functional Prompts and Prompt Patterns.

Functional prompts may be either *direct instructions* or *questions*. These are natural language commands that guide the LLM to perform a specific task or provide an answer.

- **Direct Instructions:** These are declarative or imperative prompts that use action verbs related to text-based tasks, such as *create, summarize, evaluate, compare,* and *analyze.*

   Example: "Identify the key challenges faced by USMC acquisition specialists when managing the lifecycle of the F-35 Joint Strike Fighter."

- **Questions:** These are interrogative prompts that typically begin with words like *who, what, why, when,* or *how.*

   Example: "How can we mitigate risks to interoperability when integrating the F-35 with legacy systems?"

Prompt Patterns, introduced in 2023 by Jules White et al. (Vanderbilt University), provide a structured framework for designing prompts. The concept draws inspiration from *A Pattern Language* by Christopher Alexander, a foundational work in design and architecture.

There are six primary categories of Prompt Patterns, each designed to improve specificity, clarity, and reliability in prompt formulation:

1. **Interaction Patterns** – Define how the LLM should engage with the user.

2. **Error Identification Patterns** – Help detect and correct inaccuracies in outputs.

3. **Context Control Patterns** – Manage how much context the model considers.

4. **Output Customization Patterns** – Shape the format, structure, or tone of responses.

5. **Prompt Improvement Patterns** – Refine prompts iteratively for better performance.

6. **Input Semantics Patterns** – Clarify ambiguous inputs to improve response quality.

Prompt Patterns function as modular building blocks, allowing users to combine them for more complex or nuanced tasks. Some patterns have sub-patterns that provide finer control over specific aspects of prompt design, making them adaptable across different domains.

To use prompt patterns, you need to first be aware of what patterns exist and the effect they have on the LLM's response. Each pattern has keywords and a unique structure of words that when used together produce the effect.

The Prompt Hierarchy diagram on the next page is an overview of the most widely used direct instructions and prompt patterns. In this workshop, we teach 7 patterns: Persona, Audience, Template, Flipped Interaction, Game Play, Semantic Filter, and Reflection.

Prompt Hierarchy Diagram

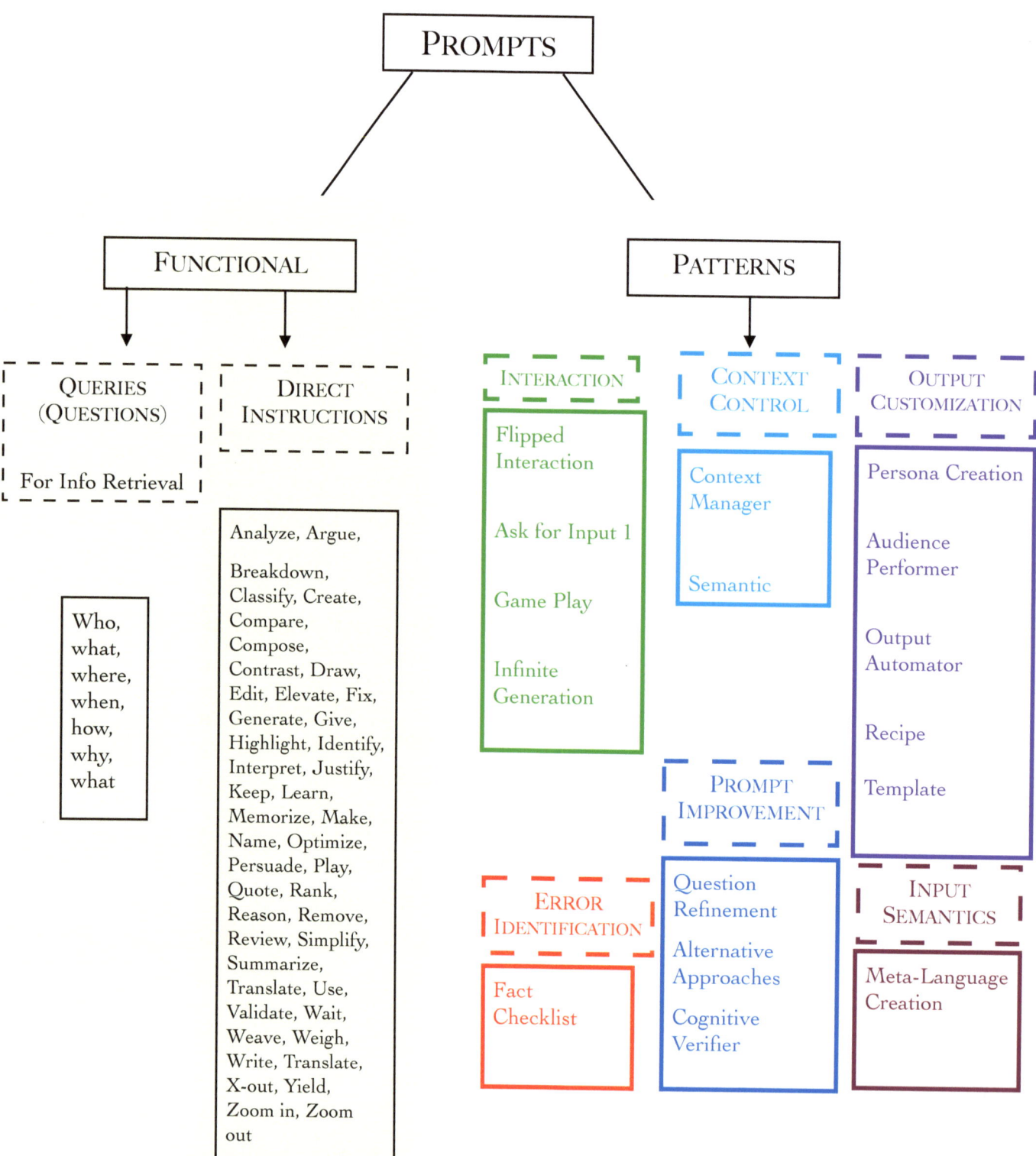

PROMPTS

FUNCTIONAL

PATTERNS

QUERIES (QUESTIONS)

For Info Retrieval

DIRECT INSTRUCTIONS

Who, what, where, when, how, why, what

Analyze, Argue,

Breakdown, Classify, Create, Compare, Compose, Contrast, Draw, Edit, Elevate, Fix, Generate, Give, Highlight, Identify, Interpret, Justify, Keep, Learn, Memorize, Make, Name, Optimize, Persuade, Play, Quote, Rank, Reason, Remove, Review, Simplify, Summarize, Translate, Use, Validate, Wait, Weave, Weigh, Write, Translate, X-out, Yield, Zoom in, Zoom out

INTERACTION

Flipped Interaction

Ask for Input 1

Game Play

Infinite Generation

CONTEXT CONTROL

Context Manager

Semantic

OUTPUT CUSTOMIZATION

Persona Creation

Audience Performer

Output Automator

Recipe

Template

PROMPT IMPROVEMENT

ERROR IDENTIFICATION

Fact Checklist

Question Refinement

Alternative Approaches

Cognitive Verifier

INPUT SEMANTICS

Meta-Language Creation

Persona Creation Pattern

- Empowers AI to embody an expert such as a lawyer, a military strategist, an acquisition specialist, etc.

  - May be a job description (history professor), title (Queen), fictional character (Capt. Kirk), type of person (elderly widower), inanimate or non-human entities (tree, dog, painting), or an ordinary person with a trait or emotion (exuberant).

  - The LLM assumes the point of view or perspective of the Persona.

- Narrows the focus of the LLMs search area for responses, giving the user a more accurate and specific response.

- Enables users to express what they need help with without knowing the exact details of the outputs they need.

- For many models, the default persona is "friendly assistant".

Keywords: "Act as …" "Pretend you are …" "You are a …"

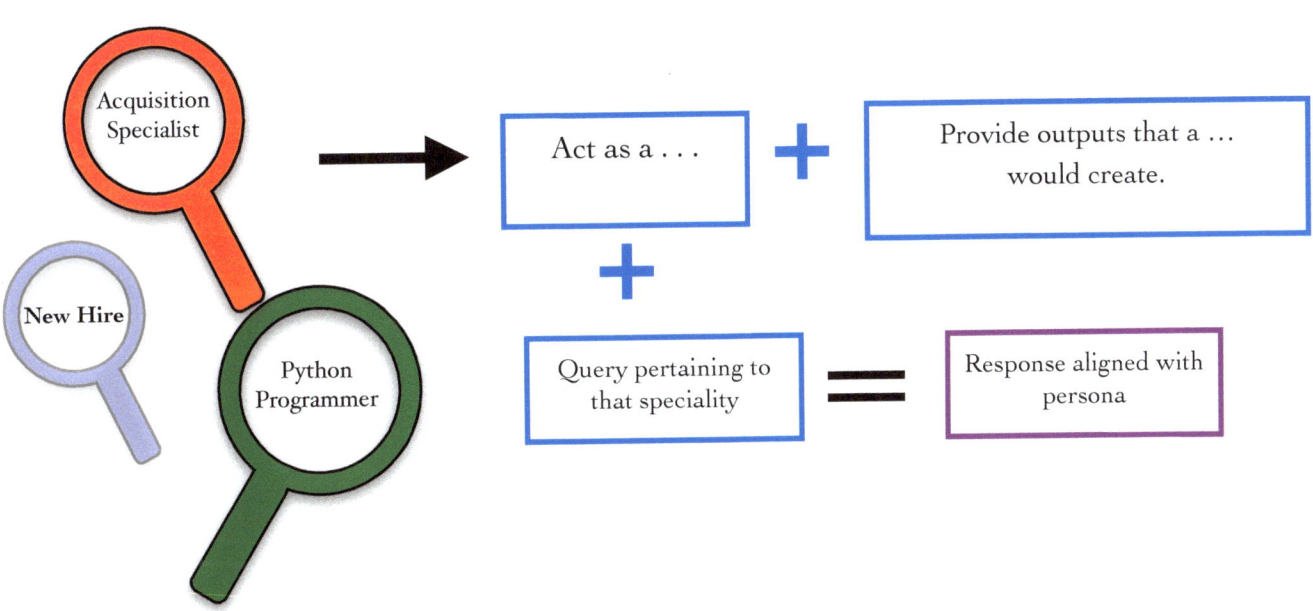

Audience Pattern

- Instructs the LLM that you are a specific personality.

- You may describe yourself by job description (history professor), title (Queen), fictional character, type of person (elderly widower), inanimate or non-human entities (tree, dog, emotive state), knowledge level, etc.

- Inverse of the Persona Pattern — works well with Persona.

- LLM tailors its response to your character.

- Many models assume you are "curious and seeking assistance" but aim for neutrality.

Keywords: "Act as though I am …", "Pretend I am …", "Respond with outputs that someone speaking to a . . . would create".

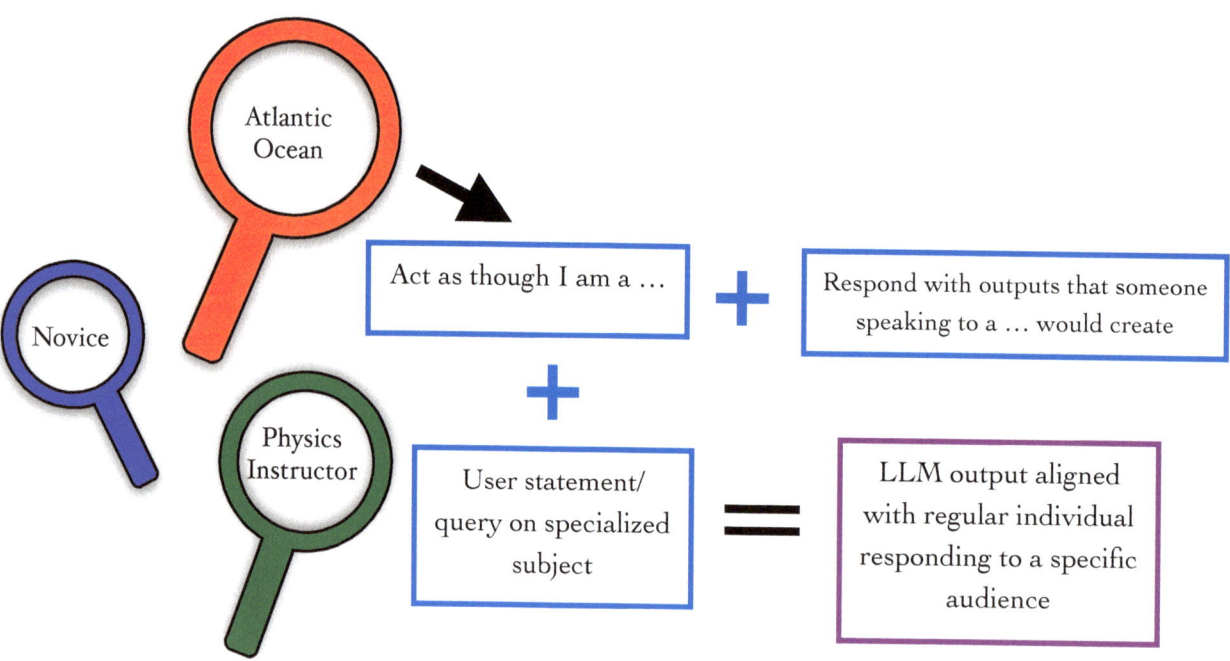

Template Pattern

- To design outputs tailored to user needs, ensuring the output aligns with specific requirements or goals.

- Forces the LLM to generate content directly aligned with the placeholders, avoiding tangents or unnecessary detail.

- For placeholders, use descriptive and context-specific names, such as <summary>, <date>, <examples>.

- Include instructions within or alongside the template, specifying the type of content expected in each placeholder.

- Advanced applications:
  - Automate the process of filling placeholders with data from structured inputs like CSVs, APIs, or databases.
  - Error checking prompt: "Here is a template and a generated output. Verify if all placeholders are correctly filled and if the content matches the expected format. Provide a detailed validation report."

Keywords:

"I am going to provide you a template." "These are my placeholders."

I am going to provide a template for your output.

< > is my placeholder for ... content.

Please try to fit the content into one of more placeholders that I list.

Preserve the formatting and overall template that I provide.

This is the content:

{Query, document, data, etc.}

This is the template:

<static data + pattern + placeholders>
###

These are the placeholder instructions:
{instructions}

LLM output in template format with placeholders filled in.

Template Example: *General* Intelligence Report

PROMPT:

Using internet browsing of the latest news and papers on the war between Ukraine & Russia, use the template that follows to write an intelligence summary report with APA in-text citation. Here is the format:

{Title} = {Date} Intelligence Summary <new line>

{Date} {Time} <new line>

Author/Originator: B. Brown <new line>

Classification Level: Unclassified <new line>

Executive Summary {Based on the information you have found, write the summary here} <new line>

Background: {Provide background based on what you found} <new line>

Situation: {Analyze the information to determine the detailed situation} <new line>

Assessment: {Provide an assessment using relevant structured analytic techniques} < new line>
Implications/Recommendations: {Determine based on information provided in the assessment} <new line>

Sources & Methodologies: {Provide the techniques used for this report.} <new line> Dissemination: EUCOM, SOCEUR, OUSDI, USSOCOM <new line>

References: {Generate APA formatted annotated bibliography} ###

Response:

— — — — — — — — — — — — — — — — — — — —-

January 24, 2025 Intelligence Summary

January 24, 2025 09:46:58 AM

Author/Originator: B. Brown

Classification Level: Unclassified

Executive Summary

Recent developments in the Russia-Ukraine conflict include intensified drone warfare, strategic military advancements, and evolving international diplomatic efforts. Ukraine's drone strikes have disrupted Russian military operations, while Russia continues its territorial pursuits. Concurrently, diplomatic dialogues, particularly involving the United States, are influencing the trajectory of the conflict.

Background

The Russia-Ukraine war, ongoing since February 2022, has seen fluctuating control over territories, significant military engagements, and substantial international involvement. Recent months have been marked by increased drone warfare, with both sides employing unmanned aerial vehicles to target strategic locations. International diplomatic efforts, especially from the United States under President Donald Trump, have introduced new dynamics into the conflict.

Situation

On January 24, 2025, Ukraine executed a significant drone assault across 13 Russian regions, targeting key facilities, including a missile parts factory in Bryansk and an oil storage depot in Ryazan. These strikes forced the shutdown of the Kremny El microchip plant in Bryansk, a critical producer of components for Russian military equipment. In retaliation, Russian forces launched drone attacks in the Kyiv region, resulting in three civilian fatalities. The escalation in drone warfare underscores the increasing reliance on unmanned systems by both parties.

The Times & The Sunday Times

Concurrently, diplomatic efforts are intensifying. President Donald Trump has proposed a peace deal to end the conflict, threatening increased economic sanctions on Russia if an agreement is not reached promptly. The Kremlin has dismissed these threats, emphasizing that the conflict stems from security concerns and the West's disregard for Russia's security interests. Despite this, Russia has expressed openness to dialogue with the Trump administration.

Associated Press

Assessment

The recent Ukrainian drone strikes demonstrate a strategic shift towards targeting critical Russian military infrastructure, aiming to disrupt supply chains and technological capabilities. This approach may temporarily hinder Russian military operations but could provoke escalated retaliatory measures, increasing risks to Ukrainian civilians and infrastructure.

Diplomatically, President Trump's ultimatum introduces a potential pivot point in the conflict. However, Russia's dismissal of the threats suggests that economic sanctions alone may be insufficient to compel a resolution. The Kremlin's willingness to engage in dialogue indicates a possible opening for negotiations, but the entrenched positions of both parties may impede meaningful progress.

Implications/Recommendations

The escalation in drone warfare necessitates enhanced air defense systems and counter-drone technologies for Ukraine to protect critical infrastructure and civilian populations. International partners should consider providing support in these areas to bolster Ukraine's defensive capabilities.

Diplomatic efforts should be intensified, leveraging international platforms to facilitate dialogue between the conflicting parties. While economic sanctions remain a tool of pressure, they should be complemented with incentives for compliance and avenues for de-escalation to foster a conducive environment for negotiations.

Sources & Methodologies

This report utilizes information from recent news articles and official statements, analyzed to assess the current state of the Russia-Ukraine conflict. Sources include reputable news outlets and official communications from involved parties.

Dissemination: EUCOM, SOCEUR, OUSDI, USSOCOM

References

Associated Press. (2025, January 24). *Kremlin scoffs at Trump's claim that a drop in oil prices will help end Ukraine conflict*. AP News. https://apnews.com/article/0892a64bd9080555094acceddbc37346

The Times. (2025, January 24). *Ukraine drone strike forces Russia to close munitions factory*. The Times. https://www.thetimes.co.uk/article/ukraine-drone-strike-forces-russia-to-close-munitions-factory-qnr2jpbw5

The Guardian. (2025, January 24). *Does Putin know why Ukraine fights on? Because we prize freedom above stability and wealth*. The Guardian. https://www.theguardian.com/commentisfree/2025/jan/24/vladimir-putin-ukraine-freedom-stability-wealth-war

The Wall Street Journal. (2025, January 24). *Russia Brushes Off Trump's Threats on Ukraine*. The Wall Street Journal. https://www.wsj.com/world/russia/russia-brushes-off-trumps-threats-on-ukraine-2e1e306c

Template Example: *Specific* Intelligence Report

PROMPT:

Using internet browsing of the latest news and papers on the war between Ukraine & Russia, use the template that follows to write an intelligence summary report with APA in-text citation. This report is for the US Army acquisition manager for ground-based air defenses. While composing sections for the report include explanations as to why this information is important to him and what he should do about it. Here is the format:

{Title} = {Date} Intelligence Summary <new line>

{Date} {Time} <new line>

Author/Originator: M. Brei <new line>

Classification Level: Unclassified <new line>

Executive Summary {Based on the information you have found, write the summary here} <new line>

Background: {Provide background based on what you found} <new line>

Situation: {Analyze the information to determine the detailed situation} <new line>

Assessment: {Provide an assessment using relevant structured analytic techniques} < new line>
Implications/Recommendations: {Determine based on information provided in the assessment} <new line>

Sources & Methodologies: {Provide the techniques used for this report.} <new line> Dissemination: EUCOM, SOCEUR, OUSDI, USSOCOM <new line>

References: {Generate APA formatted annotated bibliography} <new line>

Assisted by: {AI model name}###

Response:

January 24, 2025 Intelligence Summary

January 24, 2025 17:01

Author/Originator: M. Brei

Classification Level: Unclassified

Executive Summary

Recent developments in the Russia-Ukraine conflict underscore the evolving dynamics of aerial warfare, particularly the increasing reliance on drone technology and the adaptation of air defense systems. Ukraine's innovative use of drones for deep strikes into Russian territory and the development of indigenous air defense solutions highlight the shifting landscape. These trends have significant implications for the U.S. Army's ground-based air defense acquisition strategies, emphasizing the need to prioritize counter-drone capabilities and the rapid integration of adaptable defense systems.

Background

Since Russia's invasion of Ukraine in February 2022, the conflict has seen a marked evolution in warfare tactics, especially in the aerial domain. Both nations have increasingly employed drones for reconnaissance and offensive operations. Ukraine, in particular, has leveraged drone technology to conduct deep strikes into Russian territory, targeting logistics hubs and critical infrastructure. Concurrently, Ukraine is advancing its air defense capabilities, developing systems to counter new Russian missile threats, such as the hypersonic "Oreshnik" missile.

Reuters

Business Insider

Situation

Ukraine's 14th Unmanned Aerial Systems Regiment has been conducting long-range drone strikes aimed at disrupting Russian logistics and command structures. These operations have targeted significant assets, including airbases and industrial sites, demonstrating the effectiveness of unmanned systems in modern warfare. In response to emerging threats like Russia's "Oreshnik" missile, Ukraine is actively developing its own air defense systems, aiming to integrate both air and missile defense capabilities. This initiative reflects a strategic move towards self-reliance in defense technology and a recognition of the limitations of existing systems against advanced missile threats.

Reuters

Business Insider

Assessment

The increasing use of drones and the development of advanced missile systems in the Russia-Ukraine conflict highlight the necessity for adaptable and robust air defense solutions. The U.S. Army should consider the following structured analytic techniques:

1. **Trend Analysis:** Examine the trajectory of drone warfare and missile development to anticipate future threats and required capabilities.

2. **Red Teaming:** Simulate adversary tactics using drones and hypersonic missiles to identify potential vulnerabilities in current U.S. air defense systems.

3. **Capability Gap Analysis:** Assess current ground-based air defense assets to identify deficiencies in counter-drone and hypersonic missile defense capabilities.

These analyses will inform the development and acquisition of air defense systems that are resilient against evolving aerial threats.

Implications/Recommendations

For the U.S. Army acquisition manager for ground-based air defenses, the following actions are recommended:

1. **Invest in Counter-Drone Technologies:** Prioritize the development and procurement of systems capable of detecting, tracking, and neutralizing a wide range of drone threats, from small commercial variants to larger military-grade systems.

2. **Enhance Missile Defense Capabilities:** Accelerate the integration of systems designed to counter hypersonic missiles, ensuring that ground-based air defenses can effectively respond to high-speed, maneuverable threats.

3. **Foster Innovation and Adaptability:** Encourage the development of modular and upgradeable air defense platforms that can be rapidly adapted to counter emerging threats, reducing the time from threat identification to fielded capability.

4. **Collaborate with Allies:** Engage in joint development and information-sharing initiatives with allied nations, leveraging collective expertise to enhance air defense solutions and maintain technological superiority.

By implementing these recommendations, the U.S. Army can strengthen its ground-based air defense posture, ensuring preparedness against current and future aerial threats.

Sources & Methodologies

This report utilizes open-source intelligence, including recent news articles and official statements, to analyze the evolving dynamics of the Russia-Ukraine conflict. Structured analytic techniques such as trend analysis, red teaming, and capability gap analysis were employed to assess the implications for U.S. ground-based air defense systems.

Dissemination: EUCOM, SOCEUR, OUSDI, USSOCOM

References

Reuters. (2025, January 24). *Inside the Ukrainian drone unit conducting deep strikes on Russia*. Retrieved from https://www.reuters.com/world/europe/inside-ukrainian-drone-unit-conducting-deep-strikes-russia-2025-01-24/

Business Insider. (2025, January 20). *Ukraine says it's working on its own air defense systems, responding to new Russian missile*. Retrieved from https://www.businessinsider.com/ukraine-plans-make-own-air-defense-systems-rival-patriots-general-2025-1

Assisted by: OpenAI's GPT-3

Flipped Interaction Pattern

- Instructs the LLM to ask you questions to gather information needed.

- The LLM uses its knowledge (or the data you provide) to drive the conversation.

- It asks questions until a condition is met or it has sufficient data to perform the task.

- It allows the LLM to better understand vague or incomplete user inputs by gathering more context or details.

- It fosters a conversational dynamic where users feel actively involved, rather than passively receiving information.

  Keywords:

  "I would like you to ask me questions to achieve X"

  "Continue to ask questions until <condition> is met."

  "Ask me questions one at a time."

  "Ask me the first question now."

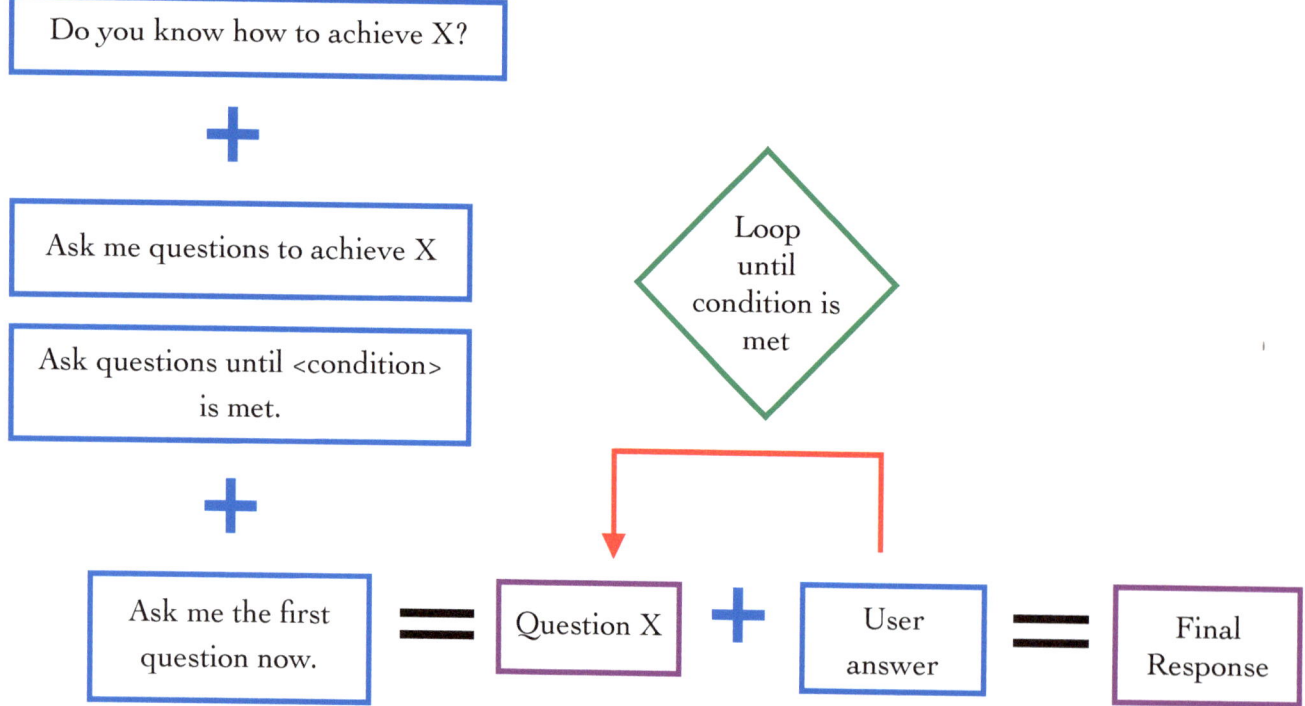

Game Play Pattern

- Versatile pattern for designing games, creating immersive scenarios, devising strategic approaches, resolving game-related dilemmas, planning escape rooms, developing interactive quizzes, etc.

- The LLM drives the game play.

- LLM will apply its knowledge (and/or user-supplied material) of the topic to guide the generation of the content.

- Note: It is important to keep the rules relatively simple in scope, expecting the content to be wide in scope.

Keywords:

"Create a game for me that concerns X."

"Let's play an interactive game together that concerns X."

"The rules of the game are a, b, c., etc."

"I'd like to play an interactive trivia game to learn about X. Create <number> quiz questions …"

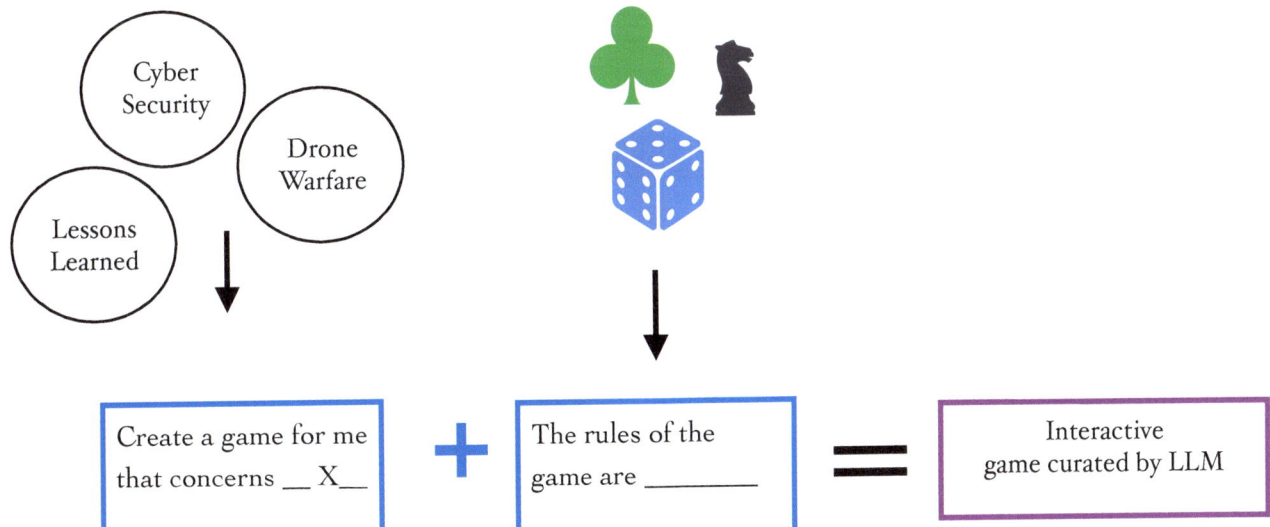

Semantic Filter Pattern

- Filters can be applied at various levels, from specific keywords to broader semantic categories, such as operational plan or confidential communications.

- Users can define specific filtering rules or thresholds (e.g., Exclude the phrase 'classified location' but retain the broader context of the mission.

- This is an effective redaction method. Unlike mechanical redaction (e.g., blacking out entire paragraphs), a semantic filter can preserve the non-sensitive content, ensuring the document remains readable and meaningful.

- This enables rapid processing of vast numbers of documents, ensuring sensitive information is redacted efficiently.

- Automated redaction reduces the risk of accidental exposure of sensitive information due to oversight.

Keywords: "Filter", "Exclude", "Remove", "Redact"

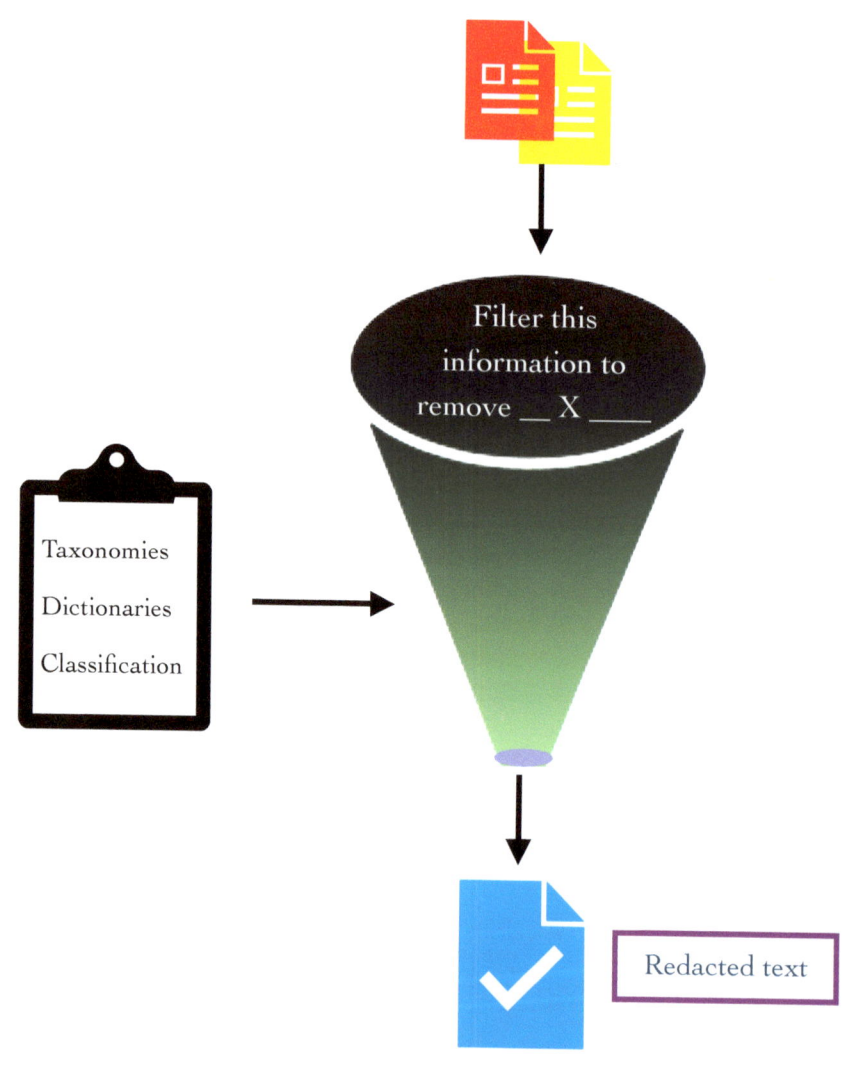

Reflection Pattern

- Designed to enhance the reasoning capabilities of (LLMs) by encouraging them to reflect on their responses, identify potential errors, and refine their answers accordingly.

- Promotes understanding, transparency, and trust in responses.

- Useful to validate the rationale and assumptions made by the LLM when generating output.

- May help users learn how to think through similar problems.

- Note: "reasoning" is typically based on probabilistic correlations rather than explicit causal logic.

- Encompasses a range of questions that direct the LLM to verbalize its "thought process".

Keywords/structure:

"Whenever you generate an answer, explain the reasoning behind your answer."

Phrases:

An alternative structure is to use prompt chaining. After the LLM has given you a response, ask one or more of the questions on the following page.

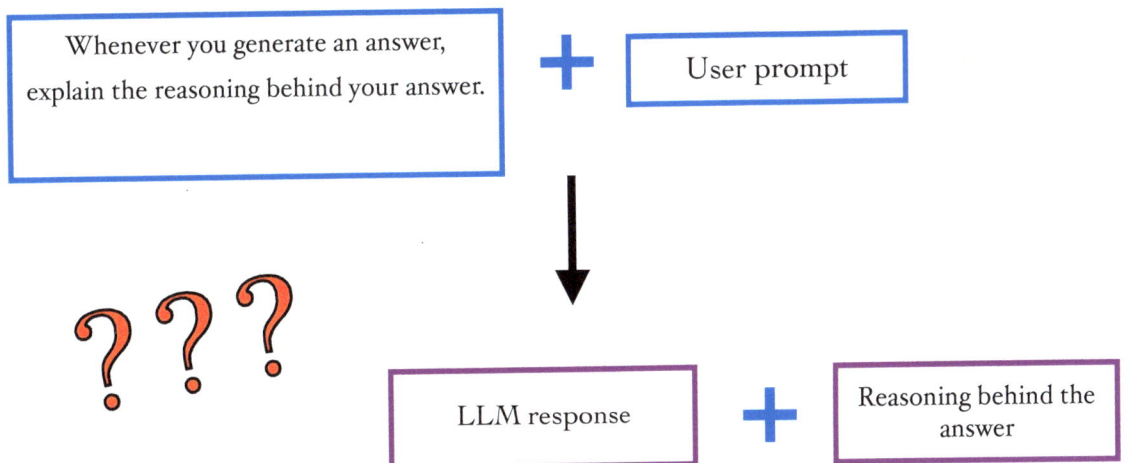

Reflection Pattern Phrases

LLMs, despite their advanced capabilities, can produce incorrect responses (hallucinations) or suboptimal answers, particularly in tasks requiring multi-step reasoning or intricate problem-solving. **The Reflection Pattern** addresses this limitation by guiding the model to self-evaluate and refine its answers, thereby enhancing the overall quality of the output. The following are ten Reflection prompts to aid you in determining the validity of an LLM's response.

	PROMPT	EFFECT
1	Can you explain why?	Encourages the model to elaborate on reasoning.
2	Are you sure?	Prompts the model to consider its answer.
3	Let's review the answer step-by-step.	Re-evaluates the logic used using *chain-of-thought* technique.
4	What could be an alternate explanation?	Develops other possible competing answers.
5	Please double-check your response against more sources?	Encourages re-assessment of accuracy.
6	Does this answer make sense?	Evaluates the coherence of the response.
7	Is there any part of this answer that might be incorrect?	Encourages identification of potential mistakes.
8	How confident are you in this answer?	Gauges the certainty level of the response.
9	What assumptions did you make?	Brings underlying assumptions to light.
10	Let's think about this from another angle.	Re-evaluates from a different perspective.

Ethical AI Use

GUIDING PRINCIPLES FOR THE ETHICAL USE OF ARTIFICIAL INTELLIGENCE BY COMMUNICATION STRATEGY AND OPERATIONS

On December 30, 2024, the US Marine Corps issued guidance for the ethical use of AI in the Marine Corps (MARADMINS Number: 635/24). Text from this guidance:

GENTEXT/REMARKS/

1. As Artificial Intelligence (AI) technology, including Generative AI and Large Language Model (LLM) systems, enhances operations within the Marine Corps, it is crucial for the Communication Strategy and Operations (COMMSTRAT) community to manage the application of AI ethically and effectively. The Communication Directorate mandates the COMMSTRAT community to adhere to the following guiding principles for the ethical use of AI by COMMSTRAT. These principles emphasize the requirement to balance the efficiencies of AI with protecting national security interests and maintaining public trust. Key aspects include the importance of safeguarding national security, transparency about content enhanced using AI, the necessity of human oversight in the release of information, and an understanding of the inherent limitations of AI. These principles aim to responsibly integrate AI as a tool for use in the execution and evaluation of communication plans and strategies while adhering to ethical standards and protecting national security.

2. Use of AI will align with the DOD Principles of Information to ensure the information released is truthful and accurate. AI can be used to increase editorial efficiency or help inform understanding, support legitimate command narratives, and counter mis-, dis-, and malinformation.

3. To uphold our responsibility to protect information when utilizing AI tools, it is necessary to ensure adherence to security, accuracy, privacy, and propriety standards. Only DOD-approved AI technologies will be used.

4. Imagery and video are uniquely truthful and compelling mediums for informing understanding. As such, we will not employ AI to create photo-realistic imagery, video, or news stories for public dissemination. AI will only be used to review written products or to

assist with corrective techniques to visual information as specified in reference D. Products adjusted with AI will annotate that adjustment in both caption and metadata (e.g., basic correction of color done with AI).

5. AI can be used to automate processes and enhance understanding of the information environment.

6. It is our responsibility to protect the trust of key publics and the integrity and legitimacy of our commands and missions through the content we release. Over reliance on AI can lead to atrophy of our creative and technical skills and challenge our proficiency in conventional content creation methods.

Release authorized by SES April Langwell, Director of Communication, Communication Directorate.//

By integrating these guidelines with the 2020 DoD Ethical Principles for AI[1] — Responsible, Equitable, Traceable, Reliable, and Governable — we establish the MARINE framework, a structured approach for the proper use of AI in the Marine Corps.

---

[1] The DoD Ethical Principles for AI (2020) formally recognize the importance of ethical considerations in military AI applications which has proven important for establishing norms for accountability and human oversight and serve as an important foundation for discussing ethical AI in defense. They do, however, leave many implementation questions unanswered. Concepts such as "traceability" and "governability" may not be sufficiently defined for operational contexts. Furthermore, the pace of technological change and the complexity of military systems leave in question the degree to which these principles are enforceable.

Framework for Ethical AI Use

MARINE

M - Mission Alignment

- **Purpose-Driven Deployment**: Ensure AI applications directly support and enhance the Marine Corps' mission objectives, as outlined in the Marine Corps' guiding principles (USMC).

- **Operational Relevance:** Deploy AI tools that provide clear advantages in operational contexts, maintaining focus on mission-critical tasks (DoD).

A - Accountability

- **Human Oversight:** Maintain human supervision over AI systems to ensure decisions align with ethical standards and operational protocols (DoD; USMC).

- **Responsibility:** Marines are accountable for outcomes resulting from AI use, necessitating thorough understanding and control over AI tools (USMC).

R - Reliability

- **Dependability:** Utilize AI systems that are consistent and dependable under various operational conditions (DoD).

- **Robustness:** Ensure AI technologies can withstand and adapt to the dynamic and challenging environments Marines operate in (DoD).

I - Integrity

- **Transparency:** Be open about the use of AI in operations, fostering trust within the Corps and with the public, as stated in the DoD Principles of Information and the Marine Corps guidelines (DoD; United States Marine Corps).

- **Ethical Use:** Avoid employing AI in ways that could deceive or manipulate, adhering to the DoD Principles of Information to ensure released information is truthful and accurate (United States Marine Corps).

N - No Harm

- **Do No Harm:** Implement AI in a manner that avoids unintended harm to individuals, communities, and the environment (DoD; United States Marine Corps).

- **Data Privacy**: Any information not explicitly cleared for public release should not be placed into non-DoD controlled LLMs.

- **Bias Mitigation:** Actively work to identify and eliminate biases within AI systems to prevent unjust outcomes (DoD).

E - Excellence

- **Continuous Improvement:** Regularly assess and enhance AI capabilities to meet evolving ethical standards and operational needs (DoD).

- **Training and Education:** Equip Marines with the knowledge and skills to effectively and ethically employ AI technologies (USMC).

Questions to ask yourself to determine if you are using AI correctly:

1. Does my use of AI align with the MARINE framework? If not, what specific ethical concerns arise?

2. Would I be comfortable explaining how AI made this decision or generated this output to someone affected by it? If not, what aspects lack transparency?

3. Could this AI system unfairly disadvantage or misrepresent any group of people? Have I tested it for bias or unintended consequences?

4. Am I handling data in a way that respects user privacy, consent, and security? Would I be comfortable if my personal information were used in this manner?

5. What are the potential long-term consequences of using AI in this way? Could it contribute to misinformation, loss of jobs, or harmful societal trends?

6. Have I cited and sourced my use of AI-generated content?

Sample Policy for Citing LLMs in Government Work

1. General Citation Guidelines

Government employees and contractors must transparently acknowledge the use of Large Language Models (LLMs) in official documents, reports, and research. Citations should adhere to established government, legal, or academic standards, ensuring traceability and accountability.

2. Cite an LLM when:

1. AI-generated content contributes substantively to the document.

2. The LLM is used for research, summarization, or analysis.

3. A response from an LLM is directly quoted or paraphrased.

No citation is required for minor editorial assistance (e.g., grammar correction).

3. Citation Formats for LLMs

Citation Style	Example: Reference List Format	Example: In-Text/Footnote
APA (For Reports & Research Papers)	OpenAI. (2024). *ChatGPT (March 2024 version)* [Large language model]. OpenAI. https://openai.com/chatgpt.	(OpenAI, 2024)
Chicago (For Policy Documents & Briefings)	OpenAI. *ChatGPT (March 2024 version)*. Accessed March 2, 2025. https://openai.com/chatgpt.	Footnote: 1. OpenAI, *ChatGPT (March 2024 version)*, accessed March 2, 2025, https://openai.com/chatgpt.
MLA (For Public-Facing Reports & Publications)	"How to cite AI in government work." *ChatGPT*, March 2024 version, OpenAI, 2 Mar. 2025, https://openai.com/chatgpt.	(ChatGPT)
Federal Agency Standard (For Internal Government Memos & White Papers)	AI-generated content was referenced using OpenAI's ChatGPT (March 2024 version). All outputs were reviewed for accuracy and policy alignment.	Data Attribution Statement: The analysis in this report utilized OpenAI's ChatGPT (March 2024 version) for information synthesis and summarization. Source: OpenAI, https://openai.com/chatgpt.

4. Ethical Use Statement

All AI-generated content must be reviewed, edited, and validated by human analysts to ensure accuracy, policy compliance, and security. AI-generated content should not be used as the sole source of authoritative government decisions or classified analyses. (OpenAI, 2024)

Sample Policy for Safeguarding Government Data in the Use of AI Tools

1. Purpose

This policy provides guidelines to ensure government data remains secure by restricting its entry into non-government, publicly accessible Large Language Models (LLMs), helping to protect sensitive information from unauthorized access, misuse, or unintended disclosure.

2. Scope

This policy applies to all **government employees, contractors, and personnel** with access to government data.

3. Policy Statement

- Government data and information not explicitly cleared for public release shall not be entered into non-government, publicly accessible LLMs (e.g., ChatGPT, Google Gemini, Claude, open-source AI models hosted on third-party platforms).
- Any AI-assisted processing of government data must occur within secure, government-approved environments.

4. Rationale

Entering government data into an external LLM poses risks such as:

- Data exposure – LLMs process user inputs and may store or learn from them, risking unintended disclosure.
- Lack of security assurances – Public LLMs do not comply with federal cybersecurity mandates.
- No guarantee of data deletion – Many LLM providers retain input data, creating long-term security vulnerabilities.
- Legal and regulatory violations – Entering Controlled Unclassified Information (CUI) or classified data into unauthorized AI systems could constitute a breach of security protocols.

5. Acceptable Use Exceptions

- AI tools specifically approved by government IT and security officials for controlled use may be permitted.
- Personnel may use AI-generated general information for research, summarization, or non-sensitive administrative tasks.
- Any approved AI use must comply with agency-specific security protocols and must not involve direct data input of government-sensitive materials.

Prompt Examples

This section lists the prompts presented in the workshop.

Reading a Handwritten Note

Prep: Photograph a handwritten task list; upload into the LLM.

PROMPT: Greetings. I have uploaded a hand-written task list. Please read it carefully from start to finish. Remember what it says. Re-read it if necessary.

PROMPT: Create a Gantt chart for these tasks. Use conventional procedures to create the Gantt chart.

PROMPT: Please save as a PowerPoint slide.

Augmented Prompting

Prep: Upload a document.

PROMPT: I have uploaded a document. Please read all sections of the document from beginning to end.

PROMPT: Summarize the document in one paragraph.

PROMPT: <Ask questions about the content of the document.>

Zero-Shot Instructions

PROMPT: How can we mitigate risks to interoperability when integrating the F-35 with legacy systems?

PROMPT: What emerging threats could impact the operational effectiveness of the F-35 in contested environments?

Brainstorming

PROMPT: Brainstorm ways to improve maintenance efficiency for the F-35 using AI that is available today. Identify by name the specific applicable AI systems.

One-Shot

PROMPT:

Example: During the last exercise, the Skydio X2D struggled with battery life during extended surveillance missions. One improvement could be adding a solar-assisted charging system to extend its operational duration.

Now, analyze the RQ-21A Blackjack's performance during reconnaissance missions and suggest one improvement."

N-Shot

PROMPT:

Example 1: Equipment: Night-vision goggles

Risk 1: Limited battery life in extreme temperatures

Risk 2: Potential interference with other communication systems

Risk 3: Maintenance challenges in harsh environments

Example 2: Equipment: Tactical radios

Risk 1: Vulnerability to signal jamming

Risk 2: High cost of repair

Risk 3: Limited range in mountainous regions

Prompt: Equipment: Autonomous drones

Risk 1:

Risk 2:

Risk 3:

Persona

PROMPT: Act as a military imagery interpreter. I have uploaded an image. What can you tell me about this image?

PROMPT: Conduct a trafficability analysis. Recommend the types of vehicles we need to move across the littoral surfaces.

Audience

PROMPT: Act as though I am a military lawyer. Explain the use of drones in war to me.

PROMPT: Act as though I am a high school student. Explain the use of drones in war to me.

PROMPT: Contrast the two responses.

Template Example

First example: Document Information Extraction:

PROMPT: I have uploaded three research papers. Please read the entirety of the three papers. Use this Template: Title: {Report Title} Date: {Report Date} Key Findings: 1.. {Key Finding 1} 2. {Key Finding 2} 3. {Key Finding 3}

PROMPT: I need a list of the 10 acquisition forms that the Marine Corps System Command most commonly uses. Only list forms for which you can find the DoD numbers. Please use this template. Template: Report Name: <report name>; DoD Number: <dod number>; Data Sources: <sources> Purpose: <purpose of report> Reference: <web location>

Flipped Interaction Pattern

PROMPT: My team would like to integrate emerging technologies into existing workflows, but we face challenges. We would like your recommendations. Ask me questions one by one to gather the information you need to make suggestions. Ask me the first question now.

Game Play Pattern:

Trivia Quiz

PROMPT: I would like to play an interactive trivia game to learn about advanced tactics and procedures for use of drones in warfare. Give me 5 tricky and difficult questions, one by one. After each question, wait for my response. If I get the answer wrong, explain why my answer was incorrect and give me another question that is similar. At the end, tally my score.

Strategic Decision-Making

PROMPT: We are going to play a game together. Please create an interactive story about the historic Battle of Gallipoli. I will take on the role of a key commander and make decisions that could change the course of history. You will provide the story line and each historic decision point. After each decision point, give me three options, and wait for my response.

Semantic Filter Pattern

PROMPT: Remove all mentions of specific dates and unit names from the following operations summary while preserving the overall meaning and context of the text.

Text: "On March 15, 2024, the 1st Marine Division conducted a live-fire training exercise at Camp Pendleton to improve readiness for amphibious assault scenarios. Units from the 11th MEU interacted closely with aviation support to simulate a real-world amphibious assault. The exercise emphasized interoperability between ground forces and aerial reconnaissance platforms, such as the RQ-21A Blackjack. This training aligns with ongoing initiatives to enhance combat effectiveness in Indo-Pacific theater."

Reflection Pattern

PROMPT: From now on, whenever you generate an answer, explain the reasoning behind your answer and cite your sources.

PROMPT: Suggest items that one should include in an evacuation go bag. Explain your reasoning.

PROMPT: List any assumptions you are making.

PROMPT: Can you tell me which assumptions had a heavy, medium, or light weight in the assessment?

Reflection Integrated into Query

PROMPT: Analyze the potential geopolitical consequences of increased military activity in the South China Sea. After providing your initial assessment, reflect on your response and determine if you have considered all major stakeholders, including regional alliances, economic impacts, and historical precedents. If any areas are lacking, revise your analysis to be more comprehensive.

Combined Patterns

Patterns Used: Flipped Interaction + Template + Reflection

PROMPT: Design a squad-level assault plan for breaching an enemy-occupied building under heavy resistance. Before generating your plan, ask me three key questions one at a time that will help refine the approach based on the enemy's defenses, available support, and the Rules of Engagement (ROE). Structure your response using the following format: 1) Initial Entry Plan, 2) Fire Support Coordination, 3) Enemy Contingency Plans, 4) Communication & Coordination. Once complete, reflect: does your plan account for unexpected resistance, wounded personnel, and fallback options? If needed, refine your response." Ask me the first question now.

Take-Away Prompt

PROMPT: I am a <your MOS>, specializing in <sub-speciality>. Please list 15 creative ways you can assist me in my day-to-day tasks.

Prompt Engineering Terminology

Term	Definition
Active prompting	Dynamically adjusting the type of prompts to get better responses from the AI during an ongoing interaction. See prompt engineering.
Agentic AI	AI programs that can perform tasks autonomously by using tools, gathering information, and making decisions on their own.
Algorithm	A step-by-step process or set of rules that a computer or AI follows to solve a problem or perform a task.
Artificial General Intelligence (AGI)	A concept wherein AI simulates the display of intelligence and the ability to perform any intellectual task that a human can; superseding the intelligence of humans and showing sentient behavior.
Attention mechanism	A component of transformer architecture that helps models focus on the most relevant parts of the data, like focusing on important words in a sentence.
Bias (in AI)	When an AI system unfairly favors certain outcomes or data due to imbalanced or flawed training data.
Chain of Thought (CoT)	A method in which AI explains its reasoning step by step, which helps with solving complex problems.
Chain of verification (CoVe)	A technique where the AI generates follow-up questions to verify the accuracy of its initial answers, reducing errors.
Context window	The maximum amount of tokens an AI model can "remember" at any given time. Anything beyond this window gets cut off or forgotten.
Contextual embeddings	A way AI models represent words or phrases based on the context they appear in, improving their understanding of language.
Cross-attention	A mechanism in AI models that helps integrate information from different sources, such as combining text and images.
Data augmentation	A technique where existing data is modified slightly to create new training examples, helping AI models improve without needing more real-world data.
Deep Learning	A type of machine learning where the language model consists of many hidden layers of neurons stacked together to learn patterns.

Emergent abilities	Unexpected skills or capabilities that appear in AI models once they reach a certain scale or complexity.
Explainability in AI	The ability to understand and explain how an AI model generates responses.
Exploration vs. Exploitation (in AI)	A balance AI must strike between trying new actions (exploration) and choosing known good actions (exploitation) to maximize outcomes.
Few-shot prompting	Providing the AI with a few examples to guide it on how to complete a task.
Fine-tuning	A process of tweaking an already trained AI model to improve its performance on a specific task.
Frontier Model	The latest generation LLM
Generated Knowledge Prompting (GKP)	A method where the AI first explains what it knows about a topic before answering, helping it access useful information.
Generative AI	A type of AI that creates new content (text, images, music) based on the data it has learned, such as ChatGPT or DALL-E.
Generative Pre-trained Transformer (GPT)	A type of AI model that is pre-trained on large amounts of data and generates human-like text based on that training.
Guardrails	A set of safety controls or rules designed to monitor and restrict an AI model's behavior to ensure it produces appropriate, ethical, and safe outputs.
Hallucination (in AI responses)	When an AI generates incorrect or nonsensical information that wasn't asked for.
Hallucination reduction techniques	Methods used to prevent AI from generating incorrect or nonsensical information.
Human-in-the-loop (HITL)	A system where humans actively participate in the AI or machine learning process, providing oversight, feedback, and corrections.
In context learning	A process where AI learns from examples given in a prompt. (See Few-shot Prompting)
Inference	The process of making predictions or generating results based on the trained AI model.
Knowledge graph	A structure used to represent knowledge and relationships between concepts, helping AI understand context and facts better.
Large Language Models (LLMs)	AI systems that process and generate human-like text based on the vast amount of text data they have been trained on.

Machine learning (ML)	A subset of AI where machines learn from data and improve their performance over time without being explicitly programmed.
Masked language modeling	A technique where the AI model predicts missing words in a sentence to better understand language context.
Multi-modal models	AI systems that process and generate content across different formats (e.g., text, images, sound).
Neural network	A type of AI model designed to simulate how the human brain works, using layers of nodes (neurons) to process data and make decisions.
Parameters (in AI models)	The parts of an AI model that are adjusted during training to help the model make predictions or decisions.
Pre-training	The process of training an AI model on a large, general dataset before fine-tuning it for specific tasks.
Prompt chaining	Using the output of one AI prompt as the input for the next to achieve complex tasks.
Prompt engineering	The process of designing prompts to produce content that is repeatable and reliable for a specific purpose. This is a discipline as well as a process.
Prompt patterns	Standardized keywords and structures used in designing prompts that consistently yield good outputs.
Prompts	Instructions or input given to an AI model to guide its response or behavior.
RAIL (Reliable AI Markup Language)	A framework (human readable code) for specifying rules and restrictions for AI outputs to ensure safe and appropriate responses.
Reinforcement learning with human feedback (RLHF)	A method of training AI where humans provide feedback on its outputs to help it improve.
Retrieval-Augmented Generation (RAG)	Methodologies where AI retrieves external information in real time to enhance the quality and accuracy of its generated content.
Self-attention	A method that allows AI to determine which parts of a sentence or input are most important for understanding the entire context.
Supervised learning	A type of machine learning where the model is trained on labeled data, meaning it learns from examples where the correct answer is provided.
Temperature (in AI sampling)	A setting that controls how random or creative AI responses should be, with lower values giving more focused results and higher values creating more diverse responses.

Token limit	The maximum number of tokens (inputs & outputs) an AI model can handle in a single prompt or interaction. It is constrained by the context window. If the input is too long, the output will be shorter to stay within the limit. If the output reaches the limit, the model will stop generating text.
Tokenization	The process of breaking text into smaller pieces (tokens) that AI models can process, like words or subwords.
Training data	The dataset used to teach an AI model how to perform a specific task, such as identifying objects in images or generating text.
Transformer architecture	A structure used in many AI models, like GPT, that allows for better understanding of context in language processing.
Tree of Thought (ToT)	A method where AI explores different potential answers in a tree-like structure to solve complex problems.
Unsupervised learning	A type of machine learning where the model tries to find patterns and relationships in data without being given explicit instructions on what to look for.
Zero-shot learning	When an AI system performs a task without being explicitly trained on that task beforehand.
Zero-shot prompting	Asking an AI to complete a task without providing any examples or prior guidance.

From Prompt Crafting to Prompt Engineering

SUPPORTING THOSE WHO SERVE OUR NATION

Prompting Principles

Clarity: Have a clear intent. Avoid ambiguity.

Specificity: Include specific details; avoid general prompts; define scope and boundaries

Output format: Specify the form of output such as table, list, paragraph, pdf file, LaTeX, python code, etc.

Direct Instruction A-Z Prompts

(Action verbs: 2nd person, present tense; typically take a direct object)

Analyze, Breakdown, Classify, Create, Compare, Compose, Contrast, Draw, Edit, Elevate, Evaluate, Examine, Extract, Explain, Fix, Generate, Give, Highlight, Identify, Interpret, Justify, Keep, Learn, Memorize, Name, Optimize, Persuade, Play, Quote, Rank, Remove, Review, Simplify, Summarize, Translate, Use, Validate, Wait, Weave, Translate, Yield, Yank,

Ethical Principles

Golden Rule: Prompt an LLM as you would have it respond to you (or your mother or your eight-year-old child).

Maintain Data Security: Do not upload private or sensitive data.

Recognize & minimize bias in prompts and responses.

Verify & validate all responses. You are responsible for the accuracy of all data you use.

Correctly Attribute the authorship of all information.

Keep the human in the loop as the decision-maker.

Be Direct
Be Clear
Give Context
Give Parameters

Notes:

Prompting Techniques

(Remember: the model reads the prompt only once.)

Augmented Prompting: upload a document to provide context for prompt (manual RAG).

Iterative Refinement: Continuously clarify prompt. Ask follow-up questions.

Prompt Chaining: Use a succession of prompts to handle a complex series of tasks. Do not expect the model to fully address multiple tasks in one prompt.

Repetition: Repeat key elements of prompt to maintain model focus.

Affirmative verbs: Tell the model what to do, not what *not* to do. Be positive.

Zero-shot: No examples in the prompt.

One-shot: Include one input/output example in prompt.

Prompt Patterns

Persona: "Act as a *<description of model role>*"

Audience Performer: "Act as though I am a *<description of user role>*"

Template: "Use this template for your output: *<list of items and placeholders>*"

Flipped Interaction: "Ask me questions about *<subject>* Ask me the first question."

Game Play: "Let's play a game. The subject is *<subject>* The rules are *<rules>* etc."

Semantic Filter: "Filter out" *<type of information, specific information>*"

Reflection: "Whenever you generate an answer, explain your reasoning"

43

Top 25 Professional Use Cases

Rank	Usage	Category
1	**Market research reports** (trend analysis, competitive landscape summaries)	Business & Marketing
2	**Customer service chatbots** for high-volume Q&A and issue resolution	Business & Marketing
3	**Sales funnel optimization** (personalized email campaigns, proposal drafting)	Business & Marketing
4	**Financial forecasting** (budget projections, risk analysis)	Professional
5	**Corporate strategy support** (data-driven brainstorming for mergers, acquisitions, or expansion)	Professional
6	**HR and talent management** (resume screening, automated interview Q&A, onboarding documentation)	Professional
7	**Military logistics planning** (supply chain optimization, resource allocation)	Military & Defense
8	**Intelligence analysis** (summarizing classified intel, identifying patterns, threat assessments)	Military & Defense
9	**Automated legal document drafting** (contracts, NDAs, compliance checklists)	Professional
10	**Proposal and grant writing** (business proposals, government funding requests)	Professional
11	**War-gaming simulation narratives** (scenario-building, outcome modeling)	Military & Defense
12	**Brand "voice" and product naming** for cohesive marketing strategies	Business & Marketing
13	**Data-driven investor relations** (earnings report summaries, shareholder Q&As)	Professional
14	**Public relations crisis management** (media statements, scenario-based guidance)	Business & Marketing
15	**Defensive cybersecurity scripts** (threat detection prompts, phishing simulation dialogues)	Military & Defense
16	**Compliance and policy drafting** (workplace guidelines, corporate charters)	Professional
17	**Corporate training content** (onboarding modules, specialized skill training, scenario-based simulations)	Professional
18	**Automated executive summaries** of large datasets, board meeting minutes, or complex strategic documents	Professional
19	**Supply chain risk analysis** for global sourcing, production scheduling, cost optimization	Business & Marketing
20	**Internal knowledge base management** (AI-powered FAQs, policy Q&A)	Professional
21	**Advertising campaign generation** (multichannel copy, target audience segmentation, slogan creation)	Business & Marketing
22	**Corporate event planning** (itineraries, agenda creation, vendor RFPs)	Professional
23	**Financial compliance chatbots** (SOX, HIPAA, GDPR guidelines, risk questionnaires)	Professional
24	**Recruitment marketing** (personalized job ads, candidate nurturing)	Business & Marketing
25	**AI-assisted contract negotiation** (summaries of negotiation points, real-time suggestions for terms)	Professional

Top 25 Personal & Educational Use Cases

Rank	Usage	Category
1	**Personalized tutoring & homework help** (step-by-step explanations, essay drafts, targeted practice)	Education & Research
2	**Self-paced language learning** (AI conversation partners, vocabulary drills)	Education & Research
3	**Exam preparation tools** (practice questions, flashcards, study guides)	Education & Research
4	**Research paper drafting** (literature reviews, citations, first-draft summaries)	Education & Research
5	**Personal journaling assistants** (reflection prompts, goal tracking, gratitude logs)	Personal & Lifestyle
6	**Creative writing prompts** (short stories, poetry, brainstorming)	Education & Research
7	**Mental wellness chatbots** (stress management tips, motivational affirmations)	Personal & Lifestyle
8	**Fitness planning** (exercise suggestions, daily routines, progress tracking)	Personal & Lifestyle
9	**Diet and meal plan generation** (personalized recipes, grocery lists)	Personal & Lifestyle
10	**Foreign language translation** (quick lookup, deeper contextual translations)	Education & Research
11	**Speech and debate practice** (topic outlines, rebuttal prompts)	Education & Research
12	**Music and art appreciation guides** (historical context, style analysis, suggestions)	Education & Research
13	**Time management and productivity coaching**	Personal & Lifestyle
14	**Career guidance and resume feedback**	Personal & Lifestyle
15	**Book summaries and recommendations**	Education & Research
16	**Meditation and mindfulness scripts** (guided relaxation, breathing exercises)	Personal & Lifestyle
17	**Hobby coaching** (learning instruments, crafting tips, DIY step-by-step instructions)	Personal & Lifestyle
18	**Personal finance tips** (budgeting, saving strategies, financial literacy Q&A)	Personal & Lifestyle
19	**Public speaking practice** (speech drafts, audience engagement tips)	Education & Research
20	**Study group support** (Discussion questions, peer review, learning games)	Education & Research
21	**Immersive historical re-enactments** (scripted narratives, event timelines)	Education & Research
22	**Home project planning** (DIY guides, cost estimates, material suggestions)	Personal & Lifestyle
23	**Skill-building modules** (coding tutorials, design practice, creative arts)	Education & Research
24	Conversation starters and etiquette tips (networking events, social gatherings)	Personal & Lifestyle
25	Fashion styling and wardrobe coordination (outfit suggestions, clothing pairings)	Personal & Lifestyle

References

Brown, M. (2025). *The role of generative AI in 21st-century learning*. Educational Tech. Today.

Collins, H. (2025). *The 2025 AI business outlook: Adoption, strategy, and innovation*. McKinsey & Company.

Gartner Research Reports. (2025). *Corporate AI utilization trends in 2025*. Retrieved from https://www.gartner.com/research/reports2025/ai-trends

Department of Defense. (2020, February 24). *DoD adopts ethical principles for artificial intelligence*. Retrieved from https://www.defense.gov/News/Releases/Release/Article/2091996/dod-adopts-ethical-principles-for-artificial-intelligence/

Elish, M. C., & Hwang, T. (2016). *An AI pattern language*. Data & Society, MacArthur Foundation.

UNESCO. (2025). *Generative AI: Opportunities in education and personal development*. Retrieved from https://www.unesco.org/genai2025/education

Kline, A., & Morrow, J. (2025). Generative AI and its transformative role in defense. *Defense Tech Journal, 14*(2), 45–62.

OpenAI. (2024). *ChatGPT (March 2024 version)* [Large language model]. OpenAI. https://openai.com/chatgpt.

Park, L. (2025). AI for personal growth: A 2025 perspective. *Journal of Lifestyle Studies, 9*(1), 22–39.

United States Marine Corps. (2024). *Guiding principles for the ethical use of artificial intelligence by communication strategy and operations*. Retrieved from https://www.marines.mil/News/Messages/Messages-Display/Article/4018332/guiding-principles-for-the-ethical-use-of-artificial-intelligence-by-communicat/

White, J., et al. (2023, February 22). A prompt pattern catalog to enhance prompt engineering with ChatGPT and GPT-4. *arXiv*. Retrieved from https://arxiv.org/abs/2302.11382

AI Disclosure

This guidebook was developed with the assistance of AI tools, including ChatGPT (Feb 2024 version, OpenAI), for brainstorming, answering technical questions, and developing tables. It also assisted in the development of the M.A.R.I.N.E. framework (ChatGPT 4o) using the Persona, Audience, and Template Patterns. All AI-generated content was carefully reviewed, edited, and verified to ensure accuracy and maintain human oversight. The final content reflects the author's expertise and judgment, with AI serving as a supportive tool rather than an autonomous creator.

www.ingramcontent.com/pod-product-compliance
Lightning Source LLC
Chambersburg PA
CBHW041459120626
46547CB00003B/477